GRAPHIC LIBRARY™

GRAPHIC SCIENCE

A JOURNEY THROUGH THE DIGESTIVE SYSTEM

with MAX AXIOM SUPER SCIENTIST

by Emily Sohn

illustrated by Cynthia Martin and Barbara Schulz

Consultant:
John Mattson, PhD
Associate Professor, Health and Exercise Science
Gustavus Adolphus College
St. Peter, Minnesota

Capstone press®

Mankato, Minnesota

Graphic Library is published by Capstone Press,
151 Good Counsel Drive, P.O. Box 669, Mankato, Minnesota 56002.
www.capstonepress.com

Printed in the United States of America in Stevens Point, Wisconsin.

012010
005661R

Library of Congress Cataloging-in-Publication Data
Sohn, Emily.
  A journey through the digestive system with Max Axiom, super scientist / by Emily
Sohn; illustrated by Cynthia Martin and Barbara Schulz.
     p. cm. — (Graphic library. Graphic science)
  Includes bibliographical references and index.
  Summary: "In graphic novel format, follows the adventures of Max Axiom as he
explains the science behind the human digestive system" — Provided by publisher.
  ISBN-13: 978-1-4296-2336-0 (hardcover)
  ISBN-10: 1-4296-2336-5 (hardcover)
  ISBN-13: 978-1-4296-3452-6 (softcover pbk.)
  ISBN-10: 1-4296-3452-9 (softcover pbk.)
  1. Digestive organs — Juvenile literature. 2. Digestion — Juvenile literature. I. Martin,
Cynthia, 1961– ill. II. Schulz, Barbara (Barbara Jo), ill. III. Title. IV. Series.
QP145.S575 2009
612.3 — dc22   2008029650

Set Designer
Bob Lentz

Book Designer
Alison Thiele

Cover Artist
Tod G. Smith

Colorist
Krista Ward

Editors
Donald Lemke and Christopher L. Harbo

Photo illustration credits: U.S. Department of Agriculture, 23

TABLE OF CONTENTS

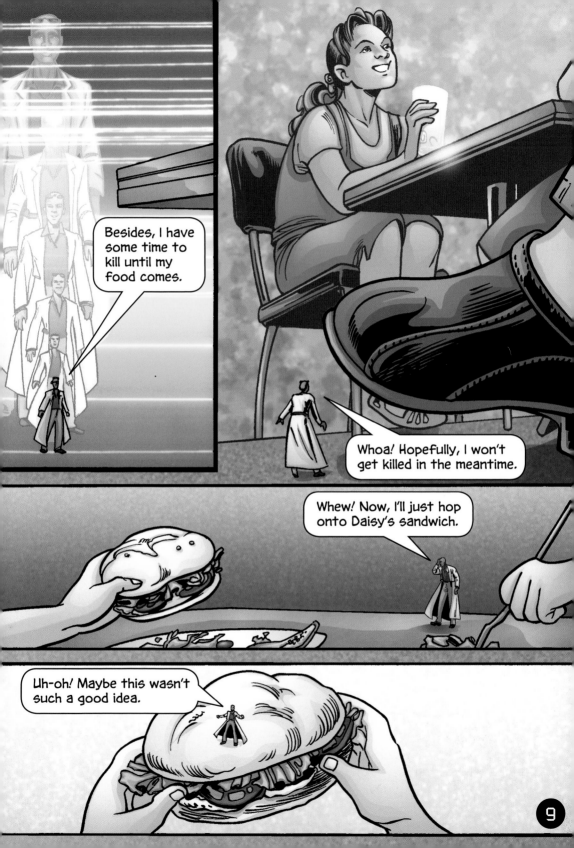

Food continues down the throat, also known as the pharynx.

Both air and food pass through this tube. A tiny trap door stops food from entering the lungs.

Instead, food heads to a passageway called the esophagus.

Muscles push the food down into the digestive tract.

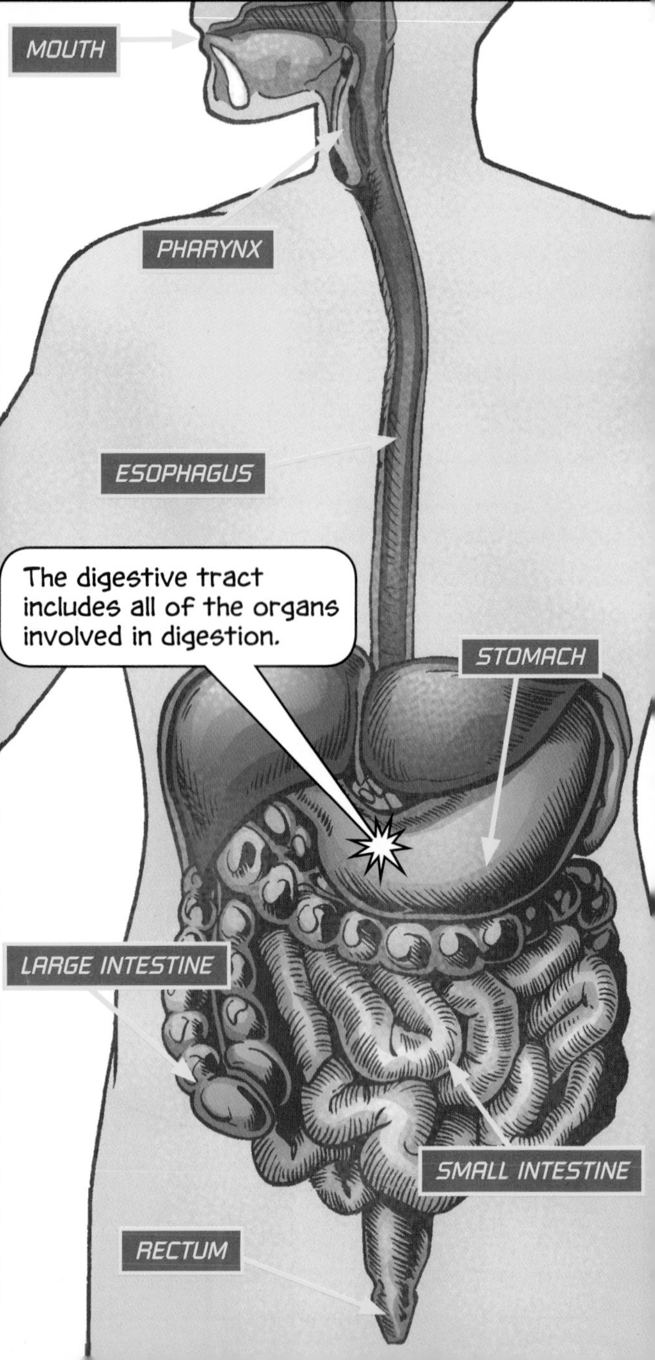

MOUTH

PHARYNX

ESOPHAGUS

The digestive tract includes all of the organs involved in digestion.

STOMACH

LARGE INTESTINE

SMALL INTESTINE

RECTUM

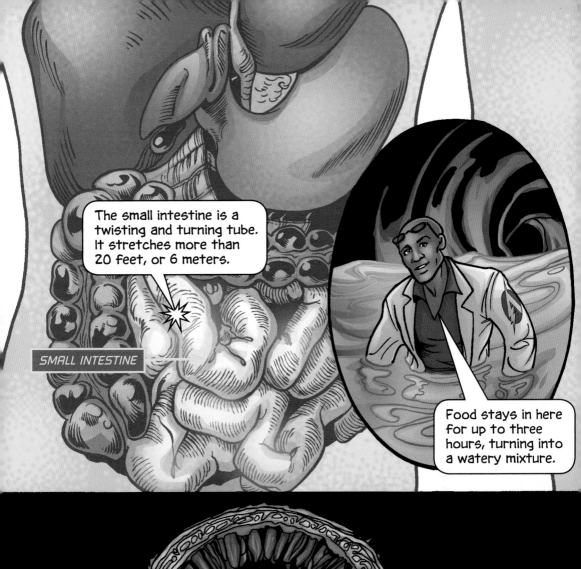

The small intestine is a twisting and turning tube. It stretches more than 20 feet, or 6 meters.

SMALL INTESTINE

Food stays in here for up to three hours, turning into a watery mixture.

During this time, tiny blood vessels absorb nutrients through the walls of the small intestine.

FACT!

The area that absorbs nutrients in the small intestine is huge. If you opened it and laid it flat, it would cover approximately the surface area of a tennis court.

This nutrient-rich blood travels to the liver.

The liver separates the nutrients in your food from the waste.

It determines which nutrients will go to the body immediately and which ones will stay in storage.

LIVER

The vitamins and minerals that it sucks in circulate through the blood and help all the organs do their jobs.

The liver also makes a fluid called bile.

Uh-oh.

RUUMMMBLE!

Bile flows into the small intestine during digestion.

16

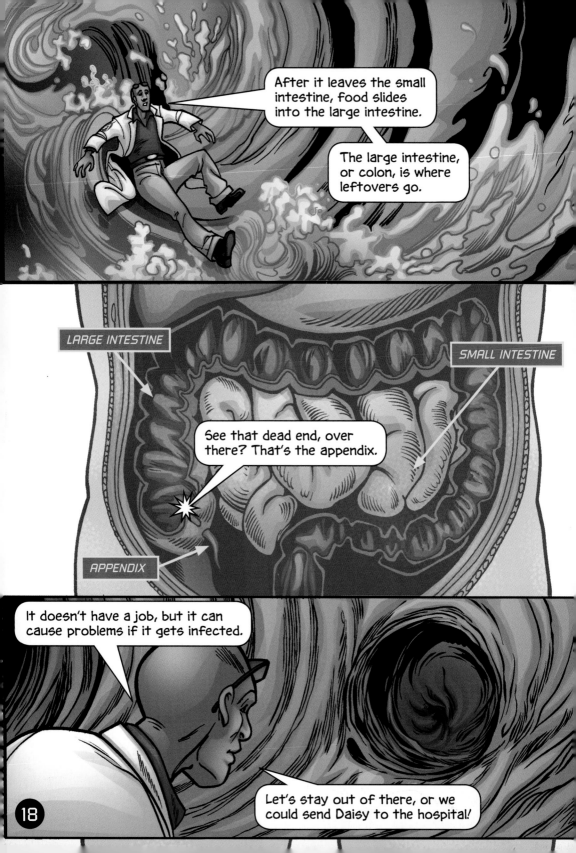

Waste that moves into the colon is a mixture of liquids and solids.

Once it gets there, water drains out and the waste becomes more solid.

FACT!
An adult's large intestine is about 3 inches (7.6 centimeters) wide and about 5 feet (1.5 meters) long.

Millions of tiny bacteria live in both intestines. They help us with the digestive process.

BACTERIA

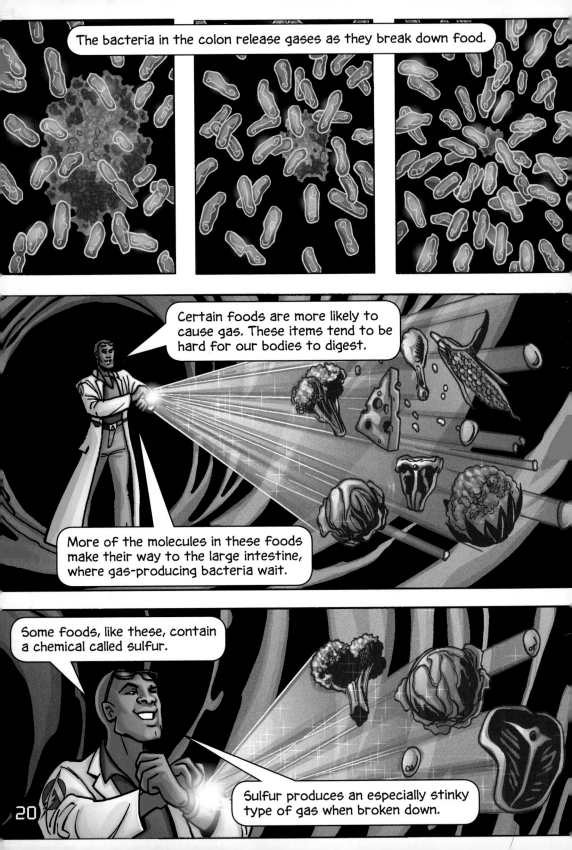

When bacteria digest beans, they release a lot of gas, but it's sulfur-free and not usually smelly. Swallowed air is another cause of non-stinky gas. It contains mostly smell-free nitrogen and carbon dioxide.

Eventually, gas works its way out of your body.

Gas isn't the only thing that needs to exit the system.

LARGE INTESTINE

The rectum is a great exit for feces.

Now, we are in the rectum. Waste material, called feces, gets stored in the rectum until you are ready to go to the bathroom.

RECTUM

But I'll use my teleporter to make a clean getaway.

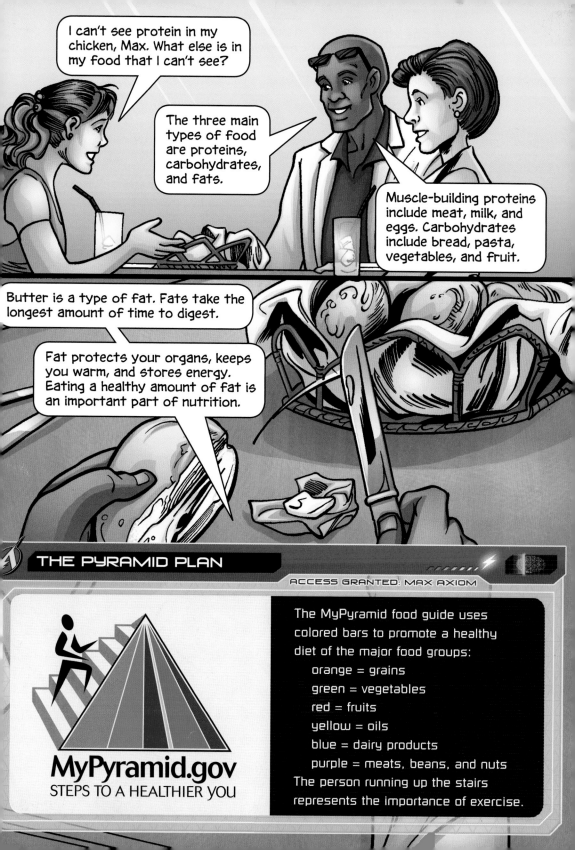

MORE ABOUT THE DIGESTIVE SYSTEM

The digestive tract, or G.I. tract, extends from where food enters your body to where it leaves your body. From mouth to rectum, this canal is 30 feet (9 meters) long.

Spit, or saliva, is good for more than just wetting spitballs. It protects your teeth and allows you to talk and eat. Police investigators look at molecules in saliva to solve crimes and nab drunk drivers. And doctors are starting to use spit instead of blood to diagnose diseases.

The average person farts 14 times a day. Hydrogen sulfide is the gas that makes farts stink. Foods that have higher levels of sulfur in them cause smellier farts. Foods that cause the smelliest farts include eggs, meat, cabbage, and cheese.

The stomach is a pear-shaped organ that expands to hold the food you swallow. An adult stomach can hold about 3.2 pints (1.5 liters) of material at one time.

Tummy growls are caused by the brain sending signals to begin digestion in an empty stomach. The sloshing of stomach acids in an empty space causes the rumbling noises.

Bacteria in the digestive system are sometimes called gut flora. The large intestine, or colon, has more than 400 different species of bacteria. These bacteria are needed to break down food to release its nutrients.

After the body uses the nutrients from food, the bean-shaped kidneys remove extra waste from the blood. The kidneys also remove extra water from the body. The waste and water collected by the kidneys exit the body as urine.

 Animals have some pretty amazing digestive systems. The coiled up intestines of an adult horse are 89 feet (27 meters) long. Cows have four stomachs to help digest the food they eat. Because birds don't have teeth, they swallow pebbles to fill their gizzards. Gizzards are secondary stomachs that grind up the food.

MORE ABOUT

SUPER SCIENTIST

Real name: Maxwell J. Axiom
Hometown: Seattle, Washington
Height: 6' 1"   Weight: 192 lbs
Eyes: Brown   Hair: None

Super capabilities: Super intelligence; able to shrink to the size of an atom; sunglasses give x-ray vision; lab coat allows for travel through time and space.

Origin: Since birth, Max Axiom seemed destined for greatness. His mother, a marine biologist, taught her son about the mysteries of the sea. His father, a nuclear physicist and volunteer park ranger, schooled Max on the wonders of earth and sky.

One day on a wilderness hike, a megacharged lightning bolt struck Max with blinding fury. When he awoke, Max discovered a newfound energy and set out to learn as much about science as possible. He traveled the globe earning degrees in every aspect of the field. Upon his return, he was ready to share his knowledge and new identity with the world. He had become Max Axiom, Super Scientist.

GLOSSARY

bacteria (bak-TEER-ee-uh) — one-celled, tiny organisms that can be found throughout nature; many bacteria are useful, but some cause disease.

bile (BILE) — a green liquid that is made by the liver and helps digest food

blood vessel (BLUHD VESS-uhl) — a tube that carries blood through your body; arteries and veins are blood vessels.

Calorie (KAL-uh-ree) — a measurement of the amount of energy that food gives you

carbohydrate (kar-boh-HYE-drate) — a substance found in foods such as bread, rice, cereal, and potatoes that gives you energy

energy (EN-ur-jee) — the ability to move things or do work

enzyme (EN-zime) — a protein that helps break down food

mineral (MIN-ur-uhl) — a substance found in nature; iron and calcium are minerals.

molecule (MOL-uh-kyool) — two or more atoms of the same or different elements that have bonded; a molecule is the smallest part of a compound that can be divided without a chemical change.

nutrient (NOO-tree-uhnt) — a substance needed by a living thing to stay healthy

organ (OR-guhn) — a part of the body that does a certain job

protein (PROH-teen) — a substance found in all living plant and animal cells; foods such as meat, cheese, eggs, beans, and fish are sources of dietary protein.

vitamin (VYE-tuh-min) — a nutrient that helps keep people healthy

READ MORE

Bailey, Jacqui. *What Happens When You Eat?* How Your Body Works. New York: PowerKids Press, 2009.

Barraclough, Sue. *The Digestive System: What Makes Me Burp?* Body Systems. Chicago: Heinemann Library, 2008.

Houghton, Gillian. *Guts: The Digestive System.* Body Works. New York: PowerKids Press, 2007.

McGregor, Emily. *Enjoy Your Meal: What Happens to Your Food When You Eat?* Life Science. Vero Beach, Fla.: Rourke, 2008.

Petrie, Kristin. *The Digestive System.* The Human Body. Edina, Minn.: Abdo, 2007.

INTERNET SITES

FactHound offers a safe, fun way to find educator-approved Internet sites related to this book.

Here's what you do:

1. Visit *www.facthound.com*
2. Choose your grade level.
3. Begin your search.

This book's ID number is 9781429623360.

FactHound will fetch the best sites for you!

INDEX